THE VOCAL LIBRARY

Italian Tenor Arias

Contents

To access companion recorded
piano accompaniments online, visit:
www.halleonard.com/mylibrary

Enter Code
5434-8915-0656-0221

On the Recording:
Laura Ward, pianist
Translations by José Dueñas-Arbide

On the cover, Francesco Guardi (17120-1793), *Venice: The Grand Canal above the Rialto*.
Oil on canvas, 33 ¾ x 21 inches. The Metropolitan Museum of Art, Purchase, 1871.

LAURA WARD, pianist, has been pianist and coach at the Ravinia Festival, and has performed in recital with singers and players nationwide. She has served on the faculty of the Music Academy of the West in Santa Barbara, after studying vocal accompanying there with Gwendolyn Koldofsky. Ms. Ward holds degrees from Baylor University, the Cincinnati Conservatory of Music, and a doctoral degree from the University of Michigan, where she studied with Martin Katz. She also recorded accompaniments for the G. Schirmer project "12 Sacred Songs," and 400 songs for "The First & Second Book" series.

ISBN 978-0-7935-6247-3

HAL•LEONARD®
CORPORATION
7777 W. BLUEMOUND RD. P.O. BOX 13819 MILWAUKEE, WI 53213

Visit Hal Leonard Online at
www.halleonard.com

LA BOHÈME
(The Bohemian Life)

Che gelida manina

music by Giacomo Puccini

First performed February 1, 1896, Turin, Italy. The opera is based on the novel *Scènes de la Vie de Bohème* by Henri Murger. The libretto is by Giuseppe Giacosa and Luigi Illica.

Set in Paris of 1830. It is Christmas Eve in a garret apartment. Rodolfo, the writer and poet, has been left alone by his friends in order to finish writing an article. A neighboring woman, Mimi, knocks at the door and asks for a light for her candle. He is pleased to help her. She leaves, only to have her candle once again extinguish in the stairwell. She returns to Rodolfo's garret. To be alone with her in the dark, he quickly blows his own candle out. Mimi has lost her door key somewhere in the apartment. Together they search for the key, down on the floor. He reaches out and touches her hand and begin this Act I aria.

Che gelida manina —	What an icy little hand —
se la lasci riscaldar.	let it be warmed for you.
Cercar che giova?	To search, what good?
Al buio non si trova.	In the dark it is not found.
Ma per fortuna è una notte di luna,	But fortunately it is a night of moonlight,
e qui la luna l'abbiamo vicina.	and here the moon we have near by.
Aspetti, signorna—	Wait, miss —
le dirò con due parole	I will tell you in two words
chi son, e che faccio, come vivo.	who I am, what I do, how I live.
Vuole?	Would you like to know?
Chi son? Sono un poeta.	Who am I? I am a poet.
Che cosa faccio? Scrivo.	What do I do? I write.
E come vivo? Vivo.	And how do I live? I live.
In povertà mia lieta	In my happy poverty
scialo da gran signore	I squander like a great lord
rime ed inni d'amore.	rhymes and hymns of love.
Per sogni e per chiere	For dreams and for chimeras
e per castelli in aria,	and for castles in the air,
l'anima ho milionaria.	I have the soul of a millionaire.
Talor dal mio forziere	Perhaps from my safe
ruban tutti i gioielli due	steal all my jewels two
ladri: gli occhi belli.	thieves: your beautiful eyes.
V'entrar con voi pur ora,	They entered with you just now,
ed i miei sogni usati	and my worn-out dreams
tosto si dileguar!	quickly disappear!
Ma il furto non ma'ccora	But the theft does not worry me
poichè v'ha preso stanza	because there has taken up residence
la dolce speranza!	sweet hope!
Or che mi conoscete	Now that you know me,
parlate voi.	you speak.
Deh! parlate.	Come! speak.
Chi siete?	Who are you?
Vi piaccia dir!	Please tell!

L'ELISIR D'AMORE
(The Elixir of Love)

Una furtiva lagrima

music by Gaetano Donizetti

First performed May 12, 1832, Milan. The libretto, by Felice Romani, is based on Scribe's libretto *Le Philtre*.

Set in a 19th century Italian village. Nemorino is a simple country boy. He thinks the potion he took is the reason for his unexpected romantic effect on the women. He doesn't know, as they know, that he has a large inheritance coming his way. He loves Adina, and in this aria from Act II sings of how sad she seemed when last he saw her.

Una furtiva lagrima	A furtive tear
negl'occhi suoi spuntò.	in her eye rose.
Quelle festose giovani	Those festive youths
invidiar sembrò.	she seemed to envy.
Che più cercando io vo'?	What more do I go on seeking?
M'ama. Sì, m'ama.	She loves me. Yes, she loves me.
Lo vedo.	I see it.
Un solo istante i palpiti	One single instant the palpitations
del suo bel cor sentir!	of her beautiful heart to feel
I miei sospir confondere	My sighs to be mistaken
per poco a' suoi sospir!	almost with her sighs
I palpiti sentir,	The palpitations to feel,
confondere i miei co' suoi sospir!	to mix my sighs with her sighs.
Cielo, si può morir;	Heaven, if I could die,
di più non chiedo.	more I do not ask.

LA FANCIULLA DEL WEST
(Girl of the Golden West)

Ch'ella mi creda

music by Giacomo Puccini

First performed December 10, 1910, the Metropolitan Opera in New York. The libretto by Carlo Zangarini and Guelfo Civinini is based on the play by David Belasco.

Set in California, c. 1850, at a gold mining camp. Minnie has fallen in love with Dick Johnson, even though she knows that he is really the pursued bandit Ramerrez. Caught by the sheriff's posse, he stands with the noose around his neck and begins to sing this aria about his beloved Minnie. (He doesn't die, however; Minnie comes and persuades them to release Ramerrez, and the couple leaves together singing "Addio California.")

Ch'ella mi creda libero e lontano,	Let her believe me free and distant,
sopra una nuova via di redenzione!	upon a new path of redemption!
Aspetterà ch'io torni,	She will wait for me to return,
e passeranno i giorni,	and the days will pass,
ed io non tornerò.	and I will not return.
Minnie, della mia vita mio solo fiore,	Minnie, of my life the only flower,
Minnie, che m'hai voluto tanto bene!	Minnie, who loved me so well!
Ah! tu della mia vita mio solo fior!	Ah! you of my life the only flower!

FEDORA

Amor ti vieta

music by Umberto Giordano

First performed November 17, 1898, Milan. The libretto, by Arturo Colautti, is based on the drama by Sardou.

Set in late 19th century Paris. Fedora is a Russian princess. Her fiancé was assasinated. The suspect is Count Loris Ipanov. She lures him into a relationship, they go to Paris, and she wants to elicit a confession of the crim from the alleged assasin by making him fall in love with her. Ipanov professes his love for Fedora in this Act II aria.

Amor ti vieta	Love forbids you
di non amar.	not to love.
La man tua lieve,	Your hand so light,
che mi respinge,	which repels me,
cerca la stretta	seeks the grip
della mia man;	of my hand;
la tua pupilla	your eyes
esprime: T'amo!	declare: I love you!
se il labbro dice:	while your lips say:
Non t'amerò!	I shall not love you!

LA GIOCONDA
(The Happy Woman)

Cielo! e mar!

music by Amilcare Ponchielli

First performed April 8, 1876, Milan. The libretto, by Tobia Gorrio (a pseudonym for Arrigo Boito), is based on the drama by Victor Hugo, *Angelo, Tyran de Padoue.*

Set in 17th century Venice. The nobleman Enzo Grimaldo, banished from Venice, has returned to see the woman he loves. Disguised, he awaits on his ship for her to be brought to him.

Cielo! e mar!	Sky! and sea!
l'etereo velo splende	the ethereal veil shines
come un santo altar.	like a holy altar.
L'angiol mio verrà dal cielo?	My angel will come from heaven?
l'angiol mio verrà dal mare?	My angel will come from the sea?
Qui l'attendo;	Here I wait for her;
ardente spira oggi vento dell'amor.	ardently breathes today the wind of love.
Ah! quell'uom che vi sospira	That man which desires you
vi conquide,	conquers you,
o sogni d'ôr.	oh dreams of gold.
Per l'aura fonda non appar nè suol,	Through the deep air appears neither land,
nè monte.	nor mountain.
L'orizzonte bacia l'onda!	The horizon kisses the waves!
l'onda bacia l'orizzonte!	The waves kiss the horizon!
Qui nell'ombra, ov'io mi giacio	Here in the shadow, where I lay
coll'anelito del cor,	with the eagerness of the heart,
vieni, o donna,	come, oh woman,
vieni al bacio della vita,	come to the kiss of life,
della vita e dell'amor, vieni, o donna.	of life and of love, come, o woman.
Qui t'attendo,	Here I wait for you,
coll'anelito del cor,	with the eagerness of the heart,
vieni, o donna, ah, vieni al bacio,	come, oh woman, oh, come to the kiss
vieni al bacio della vita e dell'amore.	come to the kiss of life and love.
Ah! Vien!	Ah! Come!

MANON LESCAUT

Donna non vidi mai

music by Giacomo Puccini

First performed February 1, 1893, Turin, Italy. Based on the novel by Abbé Prévost, the libretto is by Marco Praga, Domenico Oliva, Luigi Illica, Giuseppe Giacosa, Giulio Ricordi, and the composer.

Set in late 18th century France. The Chevalier Des Grieux has briefly met the alluring and young Manon when her stagecoach stops at an inn, and he is instantly smitten. After her exit, he sings rapturously about his new love.

Donna non vidi mai	A woman never have I seen
simile a questa!	similar to this one!
A dirle "Io t'amo!",	On telling her "I love you!".
a nuova vita l'alma mia si desta.	to a new life my soul awakens.
"Manon Lescaut mi chiamo!"	"Manon Lescaut I'm called!"
Come queste parole profumate	How these perfumed words
mi vagan nello spirto	muse through my spirit
e ascose fibre vanno a carezzare.	and hidden fiber they go to caress.
O sussurro gentil, deh! non cessar,	O gentle murmur, come! do not stop,
deh! non cessare!	come! do not stop!
"Manon Lescaut mi chiamo!"	"Manon Lescaut I'm called!"
Sussurro gentil, deh! non cessar!	Gentle murmur, come! do not stop!

MARTHA

M'apparì tutt'amor

music by Friedrich von Flotow

First performedNovember 25, 1847, Vienna. The libretto, by Friedrich Wilhelm Riese, is based on the ballet-pantomime *Lady Henriette, ou La Servante de Greenwich* by St. George.

Set in Richmond, England, the 18th century. Lionel, a country farmer, has bid on a servant girl for service, one Martha, who is actually Lady Harriet in disguise, out on a lark. Before she flee's Lionel's house he falls in love with her, declaring his love in this Act III aria.

Note: The opera's original language is German. An Italian translation became standard in the 19th century. Both languages are included in this edition.

M'apparì tutt'amor	She appeared to me all love,
il mio sguardo l'incontrò.	my gaze found her.
Bella sì che il mio cor	So beautiful that my heart
Ansioso a lei volò.	longingly to her flew.
Mi ferì, m'invaghì	Wounded me, charmed me,
Quell'angelica beltà.	that angelic beauty.
Sculta in cor dall'amor	Carved in my heart of love,
Cancellarsi non potrà.	erased she cannot be.
Il pensier di poter	The thought of being able
Palpitar con lei d'amor,	to tremble with her of love
Può sopir il maritir	can allay the torture
Che m'affanna e strazia il cor.	that wearies me and racks my heart.
Marta, Marta, tu sparisti	Martha, Martha, you vanished
E il mio cor col tuo n'andò.	and my heart went with you.
Tu la pace mi rapisti,	You stole peace from me,
Di dolor io morirò.	I will die of pain.

I PAGLIACCI
(The Clowns)

Vesti la giubba

music and libretto by Ruggero Leoncavallo

First performed May 21, 1892, Milan. The libretto is based on a court case that Leoncavallo's father heard as a judge.

Set in Calabria, a region on the southern Italian coast, 1860s. A group of traveling players includes Canio and his wife Nedda. Canio is agonized over Nedda's infidelity to him, which he has just witnessed. Preparing for the evening's performance of a comedy, he sobs about his unbearable anguish.

Recitar! Mentre preso dal delirio;	To perform! While taken by raving;
non so più quel che dico	I no longer know what I say
e quel che faccio!	and what I do!
Eppur è d'uopo…sforzati!	And yet it is necessary…force yourself!
Bah! sei tu forse un uom?	Bah! are you perhaps a man?
Tu se' Pagliaccio!	You are Pagliaccio!
Vesti la giubba e la faccia infarina.	Put on the jacket and the face powder.
La gente paga e rider vuole qua.	The people pay and want to laugh.
E se Arlecchin t'invola Colombina,	And if Harlequin steals Colombine,
ridi, Pagliaccio…	laugh Pagliaccio…
e ognun applaudirà!	and everyone will applaud!
Tramuta in lazzi	Transmute in jokes
lo spasmo ed il pianto;	the agony and the weeping;
in una smorfia	into a smirk
il singhiozzo e'l dolor…	the sob and the pain…
Ah! Ridi, Pagliaccio,	Ah! Laugh, Pagliaccio,
sul tuo amore infranto!	on your shattered love!
Ridi del duol che t'avvelena il cor!	Laugh at the pain that poisons your heart!

RIGOLETTO

La donna è mobile

music by Giuseppe Verdi

First performed March 11, 1851, Venice. Based on the play *Le Roi S'Amuse* by Victor Hugo, the libretto is by Francesco Maria Piave.

Set in 16th century Mantua. The Duke of Mantua, a womanizer and tyrant, is disguised as a soldier. He enters an inn, and as a drinking song sings this aria conveying his view of women.

La donna è mobile	Woman is changeable
qual piuma al vento;	like a feather in the wind;
muta d'accento	she changes her tone
e di pensiero.	and her mind.
Sempre un amabile	Always an amiable
leggiadro viso,	charming face,
in pianto o in riso,	in tears or laughter,
è menzognero.	is deceitful.
E sempre misero	He is ever miserable
chi a lei s'affida,	who trusts her,
chi le confida	who confides in her
mal cauto il core!	his ill-advised heart!
Pur mai non sentesi	Yet he never feels himself
felice appieno	quite happy
chi su quel seno	who upon that breast
non liba amore!	does not taste love!

DER ROSENKAVALIER
(The Rose Bearer)

Di rigori armato

music by Richard Strauss

First performed January 26, 1911, Dresden. The libretto, by Hugo Hofmannsthal, is original, with a fictionalized historical basis.

Set in Vienna, 1740s, during the reign of Marie-Therese. Her royal highness holds a levée scene each morning in her chambers while being attended to by her dressers. There merchants present their wares, she hears gossip of the court, and artists of all sorts audition for official court engagements. In this scene in Act I of the opera, an "Italian tenor" steps forward to sing this aria, which was composed by Strauss to be a response to the Italian style of music. The rest of the text of the opera is in German.

Di rigori armato il seno	With rigor, the breast equipped
Contro amor mi ribellai.	Against love I rebelled myself.
Ma fui vinto	But I was vanquished
in un baleno	in a flash of lightning
in mirar due baghi rai.	in looking at two charming eyes.
Ahi! Che resiste puoco	Ah! What can resist
cor di gelo a stral di fuoco.	a heart of ice with an arrow of fire.

TOSCA

music by Giacomo Puccini

First performed January 14, 1900, Rome. The libretto, by Luigi Illica and Giuseppe Giacosa, is based on the drama by Sardou.

Set in Rome, 1800. In Act I the painter, Mario Cavaradossi, stands before the easel, comparing the beauty of the figure on the canvas with that of his beloved, Floria Tosca.

Recondita armonia

Recondita armonia di belleze diverse!	Hidden harmony of differing beauty!
E bruna, Floria, l'ardente amante mia.	Brunette Floria is my ardent lover.
E te beltade ignota,	And you, unknown beauty,
cinta di chiome bionde,	surrounded by a blonde mane,
tu azzurro hai l'occhio,	you have blue eyes,
Tosca ha l'occhio nero!	Tosca has black eyes!
L'arte nel suo mistero	Art in its mystery
le diverse bellezze insiem confonde:	differing beauties together blends;
ma nel ritrar costei il mio solo pensiero,	but in drawing her my only thought,
Ah! il mio sol pensier sei tu! Tosca sei tu!	Ah! my only thought is you! Tosca is you!

E lucevan le stelle

Convicted of hiding an escaped political prisoner, Cavaradossi awaits in his cell to face the firing squad, relishing the memories of Tosca.

E lucevan le stelle…	And the stars would sparkle…
e olezzava la terra…	and the earth would exude its scent…
stridea l'uscio dell'orto…	she would cross the entrance to the garden…
e un passo sfiorava la rena…	and a step would caress the sand…
Entrava ella, fragrante,	and would enter, fragrant,
mi cadea fra le braccia.	She would fall into my arms.
Oh! dolci baci, o languide carezze,	Oh! sweet kisses, languid caresses,
mentr'io fremente le belle forme	while I, trembling, the beautiful shapes,
disciogliea dai veli!	would loosen from their veils!
Svanì per sempre il sogno mio d'amore,	Vanished is forever my dream of love,
l'ora è fuggita e muoio disperato!	the hour has flown and I die desperate!
E non ho amato mai tanto la vita!	And I have never loved life more!

Una furtiva lagrima

from *L'elisir d'amore*

Gaetano Donizetti

Quel - le fe - sto - se gio - va - ni in - vi - di - ar___ sem-

brò. Che più cer - can - do io vo'?

Che più cer - can - do io vo'? M'a - ma, Sì,

m'a - ma. Lo ve - do, lo ve - do.

Un so - lo i - stan - te i pal - pi - ti

del suo bel cor___ sen - tir! I miei so - spir con-

fon - de - re per po - co a' suoi___ so - spir! I

pal - pi - ti, i pal - pi - ti sen - tir, con - fon - de - re i miei co' suoi so-

spir! Cie - lo, si può___ mo - rir; di_ più_ non_

chie - do, non chie - do. Ah! Cie - lo, si può, si può_ mo-

rir; di più non_ chie - do, non chie - do.

do.

*Standard alternate cadenza.

rall. (f) (p)

chie - do. Si può mo - rir, si può mo - rir d'a - mor.

M'apparì tutt'amor

(Ach, so fromm)
from *Martha*

Friedrich von Flotow

LIONEL:

M'ap - pa - rì   tutt'_ a - mor,   il_ mio   squar - do
Ach,   so_ fromm,   ach,_ so_ traut,   hat_ mein   Au - ge

l'in - con - trò,   bel - la sì   che il mi - o cor
sie er - schaut.   Ach, so mild   und so rein

an - si - o - so a lei vo - lò;   mi fe - rì, m'in - va -
drang ihr Bild ins Herz mir ein.   Ban - ger Gram, eh' sie

dolce

ghì   quell' an - ge - li - ca bel - tà, scul - ta in cor dal - l'a - mor can - cel -
kam,   hat die Zu - kunft mir um - hüllt; doch mit ihr blüh - te mir neu - es

lar - si non po - trà, il pen - sier di po - ter pal - pi - tar con lei d'a-
Da - sein lust - er - füllt. Weh! Es schwand, was ich fand; ach, mein Glück er - schaut' ich

mor può so - pir il mar - tir che m'af - fan - na e stra - zia il
kaum bin er - wacht und die Nacht raub - te mir den süs - sen

cor, e stra - zia il cor!_____ M'ap - pa - rì
Traum, den süs - sen Traum._____ Ach, so___ fromm,

dim.

p

tutt'— a - mor, il— mio squar - do l'in - con - trò,
ach,— so— traut, hat— mein Au - ge sie— er - schaut.

bel - la sì che il mi - o cor———— an - si - o - so a lei vo -
Ach, so— mild und— so— rein———— drang ihr Bild ins Herz mir

ad lib.

cresc. *decresc.* *colla voce*

più animato

lò. Mar - ta! Mar - ta! tu spa - ri - sti, e il mio
ein. Mar - tha! Mar - tha! Du ent - schwan - dest, und mein

più animato

mf

cor col tuo n'an - do! Tu___ la pa - ce mi___ ra -
Glück nahmst du mit dir. Gib___ mir wie - der, was___ du

pi - sti, di do - lor io mo - ri - rò, ah!
fan - dest, o - der thei - le es mit mir. Ja,

di do-lor mor - rò, si, mor - ro!
thei - le es mit mir, ja, mit mir!

cresc.

f

ff più animato

8va

p

Amor ti vieta

from *Fedora*

Umberto Giordano

Sostenuto (♪ = 126)

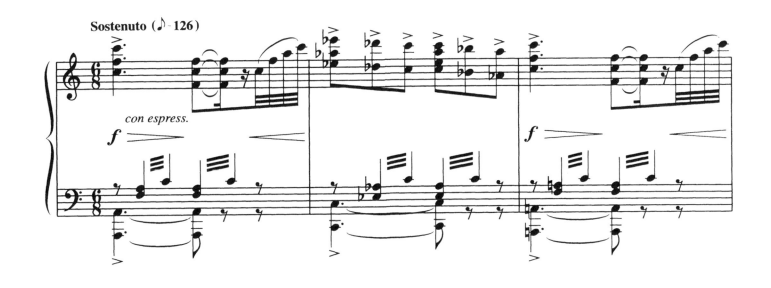

Andante cantabile ♩ = 54

COUNT LORIS IPANOV:

con espress.

A - mor___ ti___ vie - ta

Vesti la giubba

from *I Pagliacci*

Ruggero Leoncavallo

Ri - di del duol che t'av-ve - le - na il cor!

Cielo! e mar

from *La Gioconda*

Amilcare Ponchielli

ba - cia l'on - da! L'on- da ba - cia l'o - riz-zon - te! Qui nel-

p legato

l'on - da, ov'io mi gia - cio Col-l'a - ne - li - to_ del

cor, Vie - ni,_ o don - na,

vie - ni al ba - cio_ Del - la_

vi - ta,_____ del - la vi - ta e del - l'a- mor, Vie - ni, o

don - na, qui t'at-ten - do Col - l'a - ne - li - to del

cor, Vie - ni, o don - na, ah, vie - ni al ba - cio, vie - ni,

Ch'ella mi creda

from *La fanciulla del west*

Giacomo Puccini

Donna non vidi mai

from *Manon Lescaut*

Giacomo Puccini

nuo - va vi - ta l'al - ma mia si de - sta_____ «Ma - non Le - scaut mi

chia - mo!» Co - me que - ste pa - ro - le pro - fu -

ma - te_____ mi va - gan nel - lo spir - to e a - sco - se

fi - bre van - no a ca - rez - za - re._____ O su - sur - ro gen-

poco rall.

til,_____ deh! non ces - sar, deh! non ces - sa - re!_____

a tempo

o su - sur - ro gen - til,_____ deh! non ces - sa - re, deh! non ces-

Che gelida manina

from *La bohème*

Giacomo Puccini

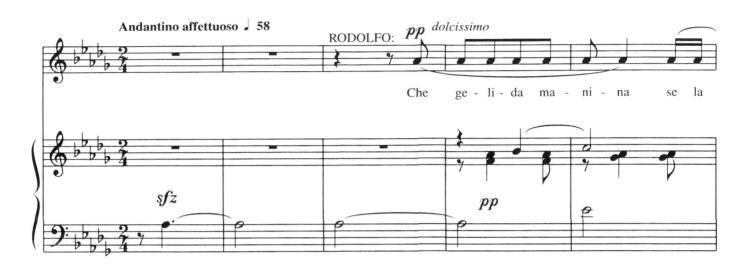

38

ed i miei so - gni u - sa - ti e i bei so - gni mie - i

to - sto si di - le - guar! Ma il fur - to non m'ac-

co - ra poi - chè, poi - chè v'ha pre - so

Recondita armonia

from *Tosca*

Giacomo Puccini

— cin - ta di chio - me bion - de! Tu az - zur - ro hai

l'oc - chio_____ To - sca ha l'oc - chio ne - ro!

Lo stesso movimento

L'ar - te nel suo mi - ste - ro le di-

E lucevan le stelle

from *Tosca*

Giacomo Puccini

Andante lento appassionato molto

dolcissime, vagamente rubando

Di rigori armato

from *Der Rosenkavalier*

Richard Strauss

51

ge - lo di fuo - co a stral.

La donna è mobile

from *Rigoletto*

Giuseppe Verdi

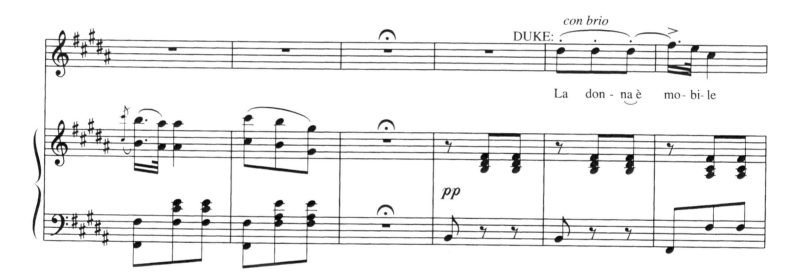

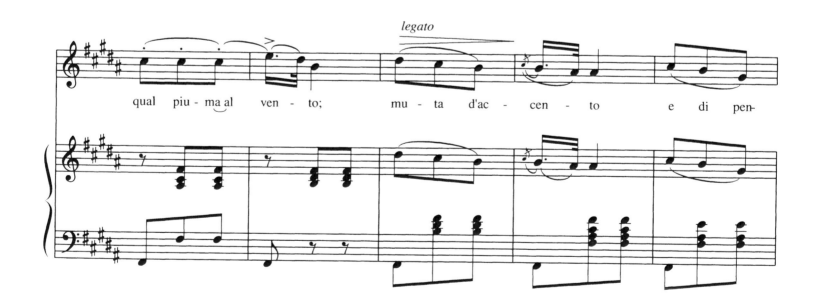

e___ di pen - sier,   e,___

e___ di___ pen - sier.

con forza

È sem - pre mi - se - ro

con brio

e ___ di pen - sier,

e ___ di pen - sier,

e, ___

* con forza

e ___ di ___ pen - sier.

*This cadenza has become traditional; begin the held F♯ two measures later than written.

brilliante

(e) ___ di ___ pen - sier.